Top 30 Examples to Use as SAT Essay Evidence

An exclusive special report from eSATPrepTips.com

By Christian Heath

Table of Contents

Leaders, Politicians, and Businesspeople:

Medicine:

Personal Experience:

Scientists and Mathematicians:

Other SAT Prep books by Christian

Write The Best SAT Essay Of Your Life: Learn everything there is to know about the SAT essay section. Covers strategies, frequently-asked questions, important facts about the grading scale, and more. Contains a comparison and analysis of two actual SAT essays, including one that would receive a perfect score, and a list of essay prompts from previous tests. This book is worth hundreds of dollars of tutoring. Makes a great companion to *Top 30 Examples to Use as SAT Essay Evidence*.

Get your copy today at http://www.esatpreptips.com/write-the-best-sat-essay-of-your-life-a-guidebook/

SAT Grammar Crammer: Let's face it – nobody enjoys studying grammar, but it's important to get a great score on the SAT Writing section! This book was designed to quickly identify weak points and painlessly teach you the inner workings of the SAT grammar section. Hundreds of practice questions and 12 detailed yet concise lessons

Get your copy at http://www.esatpreptips.com/top-12-sat-writing-grammar-rules/

SAT Math Mastery Level 1: Perfect-Score Fundamentals: Written for students scoring 550 or below in Math. Review the essential Math basics that will be presented on the SAT. Many of these topics are from a long time ago; some go back to 4th and 5th grade. The problem isn't that these topics are *hard* for you – it's that you've totally forgotten that they ever existed. Let me lead you through practicing these easier fundamental topics.

Go to http://www.esatpreptips.com/sat-math-mastery-level-1-perfect-score-fundamentals-and-practice/

SAT Math Mastery Level 2: Tougher Tricks and Skills: A step up in difficulty from my previous math book, for students scoring between 500 and 700 on the Math section. Don't let fear of the unknown hold you back - practice intermediate to advanced SAT math skills and build on the work from Level 1.

Get it at http://www.esatpreptips.com/sat-math-mastery-level-2-tougher-tricks-and-skills/

Urgent Report on the SAT Critical Reading Section: A *FREE* instant download that provides immediate actions you should be taking starting *today* in order to ace the Critical Reading section. Don't wait – this information is extremely urgent and there's not a moment to waste – seriously!

Get it for FREE by joining my mailing list at http://www.esatpreptips.com/mailing-list/

Introduction

Congratulations, and thank you for purchasing <u>Top 30 Examples to Use as SAT Essay Evidence</u>, an exclusive special report from <u>eSATPrepTips.com</u>!

This special report will help enormously in preparing you to write the SAT Essay.

In the pages that follow, you will find 30 examples of evidence that *work* for the vast majority of SAT essay prompts.

The examples are drawn from all fields of human endeavor, and there is bound to be evidence that appeals to you, no matter what your interests are.

As a professional SAT tutor, and perfect-12-scoring SAT essay writer, I've researched these examples from the point of view of someone about to write the SAT essay.

I've identified useful themes, inspirational lessons, related vocab words, and relevant facts – there's no wasted words; every detail could come in handy when it's time to write *your* SAT essay!

In other words, this special report was written *specifically* to address the needs of students who don't know what to write about for the SAT essay.

Your job is to pick examples that are interesting to you, and study them until you can easily discuss them with friends, parents, and teachers.

If you'd like to research your own topics, this special report provides many templates for *exactly* what kind of information and notes you need to take. Follow my model and you will have no trouble researching additional evidence on your own.

I suggest studying at least three of the thirty examples I've provided, but if you're really serious about getting a perfect 12, I recommend a minimum of five examples.

When picking your evidence, go for *variety*. For example, pick one sports star, one adventurer, and one historical event.

Studying a variety of evidence will give you more options to deal with unexpected prompts, and will make your essay stand out when the grader takes a look at it.

No matter how you use this special report, you've made the right decision, and I'm proud of you for preparing ahead of time for the SAT essay. It's something that a lot of students forget to do.

Good luck and study hard!

Amelia Earhart (1897-1937)

"Flying may not be all plain sailing, but the fun of it is worth the price."

"Courage is the price that Life exacts for granting peace."

Summary:

Amelia Earhart was a legendary female aviator at the dawn of the heavier-than-air flight era. In the midst of defying death in the new contraptions of the day, she found time to advance women's rights and set international flight records. Her mysterious disappearance in the Bermuda Triangle is one of the great unsolved mysteries of the world!

Vocab word: Aviatrix, a female pilot.
Earhart was perhaps the most famous *aviatrix* in history.

Themes: Individuality, facing your fears, single-mindedness, courage

Facts:

Female aviation pioneer and author who wrote best-selling books about her aviation experiences.

First woman to receive the U.S. Distinguished Flying Cross, and the first woman to fly solo across the Atlantic Ocean.

As a child, Earhart's mother gave her and her sisters a great deal of freedom; Amelia wore unconventional girls' clothing that let her move more freely; she was somewhat of a rambunctious child, who loved wrestling with her sisters, sledding, climbing trees, and hunting.

The first time she saw a plane (at the age of 10) she didn't think that it was interesting at all!

As a young woman during World War I, she trained as a nurse's aide and helped as a volunteer at a military aid hospital; before she discovered her love of airplanes, she was busy helping wounded soldiers.

1920 is credited as the year when Amelia Earhart discovered her passionate fascination with flying - as a passenger in a small plane, she knew within minutes that she had to learn to fly.

She saved up her money from other jobs to pay for flying lessons and eventually bought her first plane, and in 1923 became the 16th woman to be issued a pilot's license.

As she gained more experience as a flyer, she began to write newspaper columns promoting air travel and took up a leadership position among female pilots.

In one air race, she gave up her chance at first place in order to help a friend whose plane had crashed on the runway - an act considered symbolic of her courage and selflessness.

She married wealthy publisher G.P. Putnam in 1931, but stood current marriage convention on its head by insisting on her status as her husband's equal, refusing to take his last name, and even refusing any "medieval" code of faithfulness!

In 1937, while trying to achieve her ultimate goal of an around-the-world flight, Earhart and her navigator disappeared and were never found again. The mystery of their disappearance is still a lively and controversial topic of debate.

Amelia Earhart left behind a legacy of adventure, independence, and courage. She is widely held as a feminist icon and an inspiration to women everywhere for the conviction with which she pursued her own goals and career rather than giving in to the current view of women as less-capable than men.

Christopher Columbus (1401 - 1506)

"I should not proceed by land to the East, as is customary, but by a Westerly route, in which direction we have hitherto no certain evidence that any one has gone."

"These natives are very unskilled with weaponry... with 50 men they could all be conquered and made to do all that one wished."

Summary:

Christopher Columbus is known to schoolchildren everywhere as an inspiring and good-hearted man who discovered America; without him, we would never have existed as a nation. Or so we are led to believe. There's a much darker side to old man Columbus...

Vocab word: Despot, an oppressive ruler.
Christopher Columbus was *despotic* in his rule of conquered peoples.

Themes: Risk-taking, success due to luck, the flaws of our heroes, ambition

Facts:

Born to a middle-class family in Genoa (now modern Italy); as a boy and young man he worked on ships and as a business apprentice. He was an ambitious, self-educated man who was also very religious and interested in Christianity (and the spreading of it)

In Columbus's lifetime, the "Silk Road" to China and India - an important trade route and source of luxury goods - became much more dangerous to travel, and many navigators and traders were seeking an alternate route to these important trade partners to secure profits and power.

The ruling monarchs of the time wanted to secure such a profitable route, and the ever-ambitious Columbus devised plans to sail to the Indies to earn rewards of power, money, and fame. The ambitions of the rulers and of the explorer would eventually lead to conflict between them.

His estimations of the distances involved were extremely inaccurate (he believed them to be much closer than they actually were). Royal experts in various countries (Portugal, Genoa, and Venice) continually advised their monarchs not to support Columbus as his estimates were far too optimistic

Despite his many rejections, Columbus persisted in his attempts to find royal funding and eventually succeeded and King Ferdinand and Queen Isabella of Spain agreed to fund his voyage (even after initially turning him down!)

Columbus had a stubborn, selfish streak - for example, when one of his sailors spotted land (thereby winning a reward of a lifetime salary from the King and Queen), Columbus claimed that he had "seen a light" the night before, and claimed the reward for himself.

Upon landing in America, he took native captives by force, as servants and slaves, and showed no compassion for the harm he caused them - he saw the natives as weak and inferior to his European crew and financial backers.

Columbus made several more voyages back and forth from the Americas to Europe, always insisting that he was visiting the "Indies" in the face of contrary evidence, before settling down as a powerful governor of large swathes of the new world.

After only a short time, Columbus was arrested and removed as governor after accusations of his incompetence and iron-fisted rule, including testimonies that he used torture as a means of control.

Columbus's legacy has many facets - as a violent despot, and enslaver of natives; as a ruthless, ambitious and greedy man; but also as a legendary explorer, charismatic and forceful risk-taker, and self-made man.

Though he was not (as popular history claims) the "first" to "discover" America, he certainly was influential in increasing European ship traffic to the "New World" and was one of the personalities that shaped the history (and destiny) of the Americas.

Sacajawea (1778-1812)

"As soon as they saw the squaw wife of the interpreter, they immediately all came out and appeared to assume new life, at the sight of this Indian woman. This confirmed those people of our friendly intentions, as no woman ever accompanies a war party of Indians in this quarter" [from the expedition journal of Meriwether Lewis]

"Everything she did on that journey, she did for her people."

Summary:

Sacajawea is a mysterious and almost-mythical female figure in American history. Though there are few records of her life, she is known to have accompanied Lewis and Clark on their famous survey expedition of the untamed Western frontier of the young United States. Her presence soothed native tribes and protected the expedition during the tense meetings between explorers and Native Americans, and her knowledge of the area and its wildlife contributed to the fantastic success of the voyage.

Vocab word: Enigmatic, mysterious or unknowable.
The true story of Sacajawea's life and personality remains somewhat *enigmatic*.

Themes: Teamwork, courage, faithfulness

Facts:

Not much is known about her early life - she was a Native American who grew up in what is now Idaho, and was kidnapped with several other girls when she was about 12.

As a captive young girl, she was taken as a wife by a trapper from Quebec at the age of only 13.

In 1804, American frontier explorers Lewis and Clark were looking for native guides to the region, and Sacajawea's husband offered to take the job, and to bring his wife with him.

She quickly proved invaluable when she rescued some of the explorers' gear and records that had fallen from a capsized boat, and the expedition's leaders named a river in her honor.

Parts of the journey were incredibly difficult and arduous, including the crossing of the forbidding Rocky Mountains, which was so hard that the travelers had to eat candles to survive. After the crossing, Sacajawea helped find hearty food to build up the party's strength again.

Much legend has been build up around the image of Sacajawea as a "guide" to the Lewis and Clark expedition, but contrary to popular myth, she did not frequently give directions, although on several instances she certainly provided the best route for the voyage.

Instead, Sacajawea's great contributions to the voyage were as a diplomat to native tribes and as a translator. As a female and a native among a band of white men, she represented a "symbol of peace."

Many years after her death, American women seeking suffrage (the right to vote) held up Sacajawea as an example of the importance of women to American history.

Sacajawea is an excellent example of how historical facts are often distorted and altered to "prove" points of view or simply to tell a good story. Two of the "false facts" associated with Sacajawea: The idea that she had a romantic relationship with either Lewis or Clark; and the image that she had almost-mystical powers of navigation because of her American Indian heritage.

Regardless of history's romantic take on this female adventurer, and all the exaggerations that surround her life, she was certainly an indispensable member of the Lewis and Clark expedition and has been an inspiration to many women for her courage and skill.

Bob Dylan (1941-present)

"When you feel in your gut what you are and then dynamically pursue it - don't back down and don't give up - then you're going to mystify a lot of folks."

"Come gather round people,
Wherever you roam,
And admit that the waters around you have grown."
-*The Times They Are A-Changin'*

Summary:

Bob Dylan is one of the "coolest" figures to emerge from the history of Western music and singlehandedly brought Rock n' Roll into a new era by combining folk melodies and harmonies with electric guitar. Many of his followers elevate him from "songwriter" to "Poet" on a scale rivaling Shakespeare – he is famous for brilliant lyrics that were by turns politically charged, cryptically mysterious, or even richly humorous. His sense of style – long hair, rebellious clothing, and motorcycle-riding – also influenced an entire generation in the 1960s and 70s. Always mysterious, he both partly accepted and partly rejected his status as "Spokesman of his Generation." Yet, however he prefers to be seen, his songs have become anthems for peace, equality, and social action.

Vocab word: Clairvoyant, able to foretell the future.
Dylan's songs predicted social currents in a way that seems simply *clairvoyant* in retrospect.

Themes: Creativity, conviction, rule-breaking, not following the crowd, the importance of art to society

Facts:

Bob Dylan (born "Robert Zimmerman") started early into music - he formed and led several bands during his high school career. Although his early interest was in rock n' roll, he found folk music appealing for its honesty and deep feelings.

Soon after he began to perform in small venues, he began introducing himself as "Bob Dylan," taking his last name from American poet Dylan Thomas, and forever linking himself to the American poetic tradition.

The young Dylan idolized Woodie Guthrie, an poor, dust-bowl-era American protest singer who broke new ground with his ability to take on politics and oppression with only his voice and guitar. Dylan envisioned himself taking up the aging Guthrie's mantle.

Dylan was coming of age in the 1960s in America, a time of simmering social unrest and approaching change; race- and gender-based oppression were coming under the microscope and youthful rebellion was on the rise. His reputation at the time was built primary on the relevance of his "protest" songs such as "Blowin' in the Wind," which appealed to white and black listeners alike. Such songs provided a bridge for various movements to connect through.

Dylan's singing voice aroused controversy, disgust, and admiration - it was indeed far from a conventionally "pleasant" or "beautiful" tone; he was inspired in part by untrained American singers and by the "field hollers" that African-American slaves and indentured servants sometimes sang as they worked.

Dylan's songs often became more widely popularized in the hands (and voices) of other, more easily-accessible popular singers, but his unique lyrical style was always readily apparent.

Though he gained a massive popularity and support from the rebellious youth of the day, who idolized him and his music, Dylan felt uncomfortable and constrained by his celebrity - ever the private, introspective and sarcastic artist, he constantly discouraged attempts to set him up as a figurehead of the various movements that identified with his music.

A disastrous motorcycle accident sunk Dylan into an even further reclusion and severe injuries to his hands called into question his future as a performing musician. However, with time, patience, and practice, he returned to live performances rejuvenated and brimming with new ideas about how to play his own music.

Still active even to this day, Dylan has consistently and ceaselessly transformed himself and found new audiences and outlets for his restless creative expression. Although some accuse him of constantly shifting bases, others forgive him on the grounds that he has consistently pursued his own authentic artistic vision.

Dylan's legacy is as a revolutionary musician and American poet who demonstrated the power of song to unite and guide disparate groups. The wide appeal of his music, his political insights, emotional expression, and sarcastic humor have forever changed the tone of singer-songwriters worldwide, and demanded of artists and musicians that they address the moral quandaries and conflicts of the times they live in instead of burying their heads in the sand.

Ernest Hemingway (1899-1961)

"Happiness in intelligent people is the rarest thing I know."

"Write drunk. Edit sober."

Summary:

Ernest Hemingway was a profoundly gifted American writer whose adventurous and troubled life seemed a reflection of the characters and stories he wrote. He covered multiple wars as a journalist, and was wounded in combat. His writing is direct and honest, and brings the reader face to face with themes like love, death, honor, and war. Hemingway suffered from alcoholism and committed suicide in his country home in Idaho at the height of his fame.

Vocab word: Correspondent, an on-the-scenes news reporter.
The mortal danger Hemingway faced as a war correspondent is incorporated into his stories.

Themes: Creativity, honesty, success doesn't cause happiness, the flaws of our heros

Facts:

Hemingway was born to respected, educated parents in Chicago. From a young age he loved nature and the outdoors, a passion that would remain with him throughout his life. In particular he liked isolated, distant areas with few people around.

In high school, Hemingway wrote and edited for the school newspaper; after graduating he was a journalist for the Kansas City Star. Here he learned (from the newspaper's style guide) the basic style that would become his trademark: "Use short sentences. Use short first paragraphs. Use vigorous English. Be positive, not negative."

When World War I arrived, Hemingway enlisted as an ambulance driver and was stationed at the Italian Front, where he witnessed horrific scenes of violence and destruction. During the war, Hemingway was badly wounded by mortar fire; despite his wounds, he carried another soldier to safety, for which the Italian government awarded him a medal for bravery.

After returning from the war, Hemingway returned to work as journalist, got married, and moved to Paris. At the time Paris was filled with artists and writers who would later become legends, such as James Joyce, Gertrude Stein, and Pablo Picasso - Hemingway met and rubbed shoulders with other greats in the streets and cafes of Paris.

Hemingway's first novel, *The Sun Also Rises*, gained enormous popularity for its portrayal of "the Lost Generation" that had been devastated by the violence and carnage of World War I. It was admired for its honest and realistic portrayals and the authenticity of its characters - traits that would forever be associated with Hemingway's fiction writing. A few of his other famous titles (there are many more) include *A Farewell to Arms, For Whom the Bell Tolls,* and *The Old Man and the Sea.*

In the 1950s, while traveling in Africa, Hemingway was wounded in two back-to-back plane crashes and suffered severe injuries. Already a frequent drinker, Hemingway became an alcoholic to combat the physical pain he suffered from.

His health began to deteriorate quickly, along with his mental faculties; he was admitted to a clinic for treatment of hypertension, and other hidden psychological problems were becoming apparent.

In 1961, Hemingway, like his father before him, committed suicide at his home in Ketchum, Idaho. Contributing causes were probably his alcoholism, his physical pain, and bipolar disorder.

Major themes in Hemingway's work are masculinity, right and wrong, death and fate, duty, and physical and psychological scars from past conflicts. There are clear parallels between his personal life and the topics he primarily focused on in his literature.

Hemingway's legacy is as an author and man who confronted both the ugly and the beautiful truths of life head-on, an artist who valued authenticity and honesty above all things, and as a troubled genius living an isolated life with few personal connections.

Frank Lloyd Wright (1867-1959)

"Every great architect is - necessarily - a great poet. He must be a great original interpreter of his time, his day, his age."

"Early in my career, I had to choose between an honest arrogance and a hypercritical humility. I deliberately choose an honest arrogance, and I've never been sorry."

Summary:

Frank Lloyd Wright was an arrogant, selfish spendthrift that just happened to design some of the most beautiful and original buildings in the history of architecture. His homes and buildings reflect a harmonious union of nature and design that sits comfortably amidst the surroundings. His financial and romantic troubles often interfered with his work, and he frequently endured frustrations and setbacks. Despite his personal difficulties, he managed to construct dozens of beautiful buildings, and single-handedly opened up new vistas for American architecture.

Vocab word: Imperious, arrogant or overbearing.
Wright treated his architectural clients in an arrogant and *imperious* manner.

Themes: Creativity, arrogance, inspiration, triumph over adversity, leadership, flaws of our heroes

Facts:

As a child, his favorite toys were a set of building blocks that his mother gave him (she claimed later that she knew he would build great buildings one day).

Although young Frank enrolled in both high school and college, there is no evidence that he actually graduated with a degree from either institution.

As a young man, he arrived in Chicago looking for work in architecture, and benefited from the great rebuilding and expansion of the city because of the Great Chicago Fire early in the decade, which had ravaged the city's buildings.

From the start, Wright had a big ego, and would leverage his talents for more money, or display a lack of respect, even contempt, for his employees and for the society he lived in. For example, while employed by an architecture firm under a five-year contract, Wright broke his word not to design houses for anyone outside the firm, and was fired from the firm as a consequence.

His ego also prompted an inability to control his spending, and he would battle against his overspending on clothes, cars, and luxuries for his whole life, constantly going into debt in order to indulge himself.

Although he married and had children, he flirted shamelessly and became involved with other women; the resulting gossip and scandals prevented him from practicing architecture in many parts of the United States, although Wright remained unrepentant for his infidelity. He moved to Europe to escape his family for a year before returning to the U.S.

Wright suffered back-to-back personal disasters when the home he had designed for himself was partially burned down twice - once by a servant who also committed a multiple murder of the housekeepers. In the second fire, Wright lost a treasured collection of Japanese prints that he considered "invaluable."

As a life-long admirer and collector of Japanese prints, Wright is remembered for bridging Eastern and Western artistic philosophies.

Despite his many personal and financial setbacks, Wright continued to build and develop his style, seeking a greater unification between human design and the beauty of nature. His ideas about fitting architecture into the landscape were revolutionary and much-imitated.

Wright eventually took on over thirty apprentices, who lived at his home and developed their styles alongside him. This teaching position furthered his influence over the next generation of American architects.

One of the concepts for which Wright is most remembered among architects: that the architect should also be interior designer, decorator, furniture designer, and art dealer - he controlled every element of his homes and buildings down to the smallest detail.

His legacy is as a restless, brilliant creator who always pursued his own ambitions and disregarded convention constantly, sometimes at the expense of those who cared about and admired him. His innovations in the field of architecture are far-reaching and he is generally considered the greatest master of American architecture.

Napoleon Hill (1883-1970) and *Think and Grow Rich*

"Do not wait; the time will never be "just right." Start where you stand, and work with whatever tools you may have at your command, and better tools will be found as you go along."

"Every adversity, every failure, every heartache carries with it the seed on an equal or greater benefit."

"Whatever the mind of man can conceive and believe, it can achieve."

Summary:

Napoleon Hill's created an entirely new field of authorship now known as "self-help." Hill, who grew up during the Great Depression, went on a 20-year quest to research and document "the principles of success" that led some men and women to overcome every obstacle and achieve their goals of fortune or fame. He organized his findings into a manifesto that teaches self-discipline, perseverance, creativity, and cooperation. *Think and Grow Rich* has sold more than 20 million copies, proving that Hill's principles of success worked even in his own life.

Vocab word: Eminence, fame, distinction, honor.
Napoleon Hill interviewed *eminent* businesspeople, creative minds, and spiritual leaders.

Themes: Perseverance, creativity, focus, perfection is not required for success, setting goals

Facts: Born in a tiny cabin in the mountains; he lost his mother at a young age. When he was only 13, he began to write as a local reporter for small-town newspapers in the area.

Hill entered law school with the savings from his reporting jobs, but could not complete his course of study due to financial difficulties.

He returned to writing articles, and in 1908 was given the assignment of interviewing Andrew Carnegie, a rags-to-riches "self-made man" and industrialist, and one of the most fantastically wealthy and powerful men of the era. This meeting was later identified as a turning-point in Hill's life.

Carnegie gave Hill the task of discovering and summarizing the laws that governed "success" - as someone with a vast amount of success himself, Carnegie believed that the rules and processes of success could be researched and explained, and that anyone had the power to succeed at whatever goals they set for themselves.

Hill spent more than two decades researching and interviewing hundreds of the most successful (financially and otherwise) men and women of his time, and began to notice specific patterns and commonalities among those who had "succeeded," traits that distinguished them from "failures," and skills that "failures" definitely lacked.

One of the most remarkable stories that Hill collected was that of his own son, Blair, who was born without ears or the ability to hear. Though doctors said that Blair would never hear at all, both Hill and his son were determined to prove them wrong, and eventually discovered methods that allowed Blair to hear and communicate. Blair Hill went on to be an inspiration to deaf people around the world and helped improve the development of hearing aids.

Hill took the information and theories he had gathered and refined them into several books, the most popular of which is called *Think and Grow Rich*. This book, which explained his "Philosophy of Success" in concrete terms, with step-by-step instructions, is one of the best-selling books of all time (more than 20 *million* copies have been sold, a staggering number) and is still popular today. Despite the title, the book is not only a manual for how to achieve great financial success, but success in any calling - be it art, sports, or agriculture.

One of the most fascinating features of this book is that Hill constantly hints at a hidden secret of success that he never reveals outright - he believed that "giving it away" would not, in fact, help the reader succeed, and that the effort to discover, understand, and apply this "secret" would in itself help a reader develop skills necessary to success such as self-determination, persistence, and clear understanding.

Key concepts of Hill's philosophy were specific goal-setting, using the power of desire as fuel to achieve great things, cooperation, harmony, sharing of knowledge, the idea of abundance - that "there is enough success to go around for everybody" - and the defeat of personal fears. He also emphasized and popularized the idea that one was only a "failure" if they refused to go on after a setback; he believed that every difficulty has the seeds of an equal success within it, if we only persevere.

Hill's legacy is as one of the most motivational authors and philosophers in history; he almost single-handedly founded the field of self-improvement literature and helped popularize the idea that every man and woman can achieve their dreams if they believe in themselves and take constant action. In fact, I myself would credit *Think and Grow Rich* as a direct influence that helped me come up with the idea to write this book, and to follow-through daily to take the necessary steps to complete my work. I can't recommend this book highly enough to ambitious readers of any age!

Vincent van Gogh (1853-1890)

"He transformed the pain of his tormented life into ecstatic beauty." [Richard Curtis]

"For me, the work [of painting] is an absolute necessity. I cannot put it off; I don't care for anything else." [Vincent van Gogh]

Summary:

Van Gogh is the poster child for the "tortured artist;" he battled depression and suicidal madness while creating beautiful, inspired paintings that burst with colors. His life was never easy, and he suffered through poverty and sickness constantly. He did very poorly in love, as well, and experienced several significant romantic rejections. Unable to endure his suffering any longer, he cut his own life short by shooting himself at the age of 47.

Vocab word: Neurosis, a type of mental disorder often characterized by depression, fear, and anger. It is likely that van Gogh's creativity arose, in part, from his various *neuroses*.

Themes: Creativity, success and failure, giving up in the face of difficulty, dealing with adversity, inspiration

Facts:

A serious and quiet child whose interest in art began at an early age, possibly as a way to bring some brightness and joy into a childhood he later characterized as "gloomy and cold and sterile."

In his early twenties, van Gogh was doing well financially (as an art dealer) and was content with his life. He fell in love with a young lady but she rejected him after he confessed his feelings.

Perhaps because of this unhappiness, he began to become surly and resentful at his work, making it obvious to his customers that he did not approve of their buying and selling fine art like it was simple furniture. Van Gogh believed that art was something important and special that deserved more respect than his customers gave it, and he lost his job soon afterwards as a result.

Vincent became more and more serious about religion and Christianity, and in his later twenties he believed he had found his calling as a preacher and a missionary. He lived in poor conditions and eventually was dismissed from this position as well, for "undermining the dignity of the priesthood."

Luckily he had been continually drawing during these difficult times and had more than enough talent and skill to enroll in a Belgian school of art, where he further developed his observational and technical skills.

After leaving school, his love woes grew worse even as his artistic powers grew stronger. His financial situation was not good, his health was poor, and he battled depression, slowly giving in to the abuse of absinthe, a powerful alcoholic beverage (also known, perhaps incorrectly, as a hallucinogen) that was popular among artists and bohemians at the time.

Van Gogh was always taking in new influences - including Japanese and other European artists from the past and present - and incorporating them into his own style. His works frequently burst with vivid, unique colors and every scene and still-life was filled with character.

In his later years, van Gogh hoped for a utopian collective of artists - an impossible dream that surely added even more pressure and dissatisfaction to his troubled life. His many personal problems and health issues compounded his unhappiness, and he began to seem like a madman to those who knew him.

In one of the most famous incidents of his life, van Gogh confronted Paul Gauguin, a friend and fellow artist, with a razor blade - when Gauguin fled the scene, van Gogh cut off a piece of his own ear before stumbling home and falling unconscious. Soon afterwards, Vincent committed himself to an asylum, where he continued to paint.

After leaving the asylum, his mental illnesses worsened and Vincent attempted suicide by shooting himself in the chest in the middle of a field outside town. Somehow he survived his wound and staggered back into town for treatment, but died hours later from infection.

His legacy is as a troubled, bohemian artist with a groundbreaking modern style that inspired generations of followers. His lifelong unhappiness is nearly as famous as his art, and many hold up van Gogh as a prime example of the price (in sanity) of great creativity.

Bethany Hamilton (1990-present)

"Courage, sacrifice, determination, commitment, toughness, heart, talent, guts. That's what little girls are made of; the heck with sugar and spice."

"People can do whatever they want if they just set their heart to it, and just never give up, and just go out there and do it."

Summary:

Bethany Hamilton is a young female surfer who has showed unbelievable perseverance and skill by not only surviving a shark attack that took her entire left arm, but also returning to the waves to place at the top of international women's surfing competitions. She's also used her celebrity to start the "Friends of Bethany" foundation, which raises money for amputees and shark-attack victims.

Vocab word: Doggedness, tenacity, stubbornly refusing to give up.
A shark attack was not enough to overcome Bethany's natural *doggedness*.

Themes: Determination, single-mindedness, courage, triumph over adversity, generosity

Facts:

A young American professional surfer

She already deserves credit for being a female surfer in a sport that is mainly men.

At the age of 13, she became famous for surviving a shark attack in 2003 that took her left arm and almost cost her life.

If the shark had bitten two inches farther, she certainly would have died - as it was, she lost 60% of her blood.

Her quick-thinking friends helped save her life that day!

Hamilton was so determined to return to surfing that in less than a month she was back on her board again.

After relearning how to surf with only one arm, she went back to competing professionally.

In 2005, she took 1st place in a surfing competition that she had been trying to win since she lost her arm. In 2008 she took 2nd place in an international competition against some of the world's best female surfers.

Her story has been told in books and a documentary film, as well as on television talk shows. Hamilton also launched her own foundation, "Friends of Bethany," which supports shark-attack victims and amputees. Her goal is to be a role model, inspirational figure, and champion athlete.

Her legacy (although she's still young) will certainly be one of triumph in the face of adversity, the power of passion and conviction, and the strength of the human spirit in the face of disaster.

Billie Jean King (1943-present)

"I wanted to use sports for social change."

"Champions keep playing until they get it right."

Summary:

Billie Jean King is a legend of female sports and a remarkably skilled tennis champion. Though her successes on the court in regular competition are historical in their own right, she is most famous for winning the "Battle of the Sexes," an internationally-publicized showdown between King and former top male player Bobby Riggs. She publicly defeated him in a well-fought match, and permanently advanced the respect accorded to female athletes. King is also famous as a gay-rights figure; she endured a public "outing" that almost ended her career, but she has since become a hero and figurehead in the gay community.

Vocab word: Vanguard, the first into battle.
Billie Jean King is now seen as part of the gay rights and feminist *vanguard*.

Themes: Courage, the individual vs. society, leadership, risk-taking, overcoming obstacles, keeping secrets, champions and heroes

Facts:

A legendary female professional tennis player from the United States

Raised by a conservative religious family

Got married at a young age before realizing that she was attracted to women

She was the first well-known professional female athlete to come out as a lesbian, or rather to be publicly "outed" by somebody else - King didn't feel prepared for this personal information to become public.

Because of this public revelation, she lost millions of dollars in athletic endorsements and struggled through protracted and expensive legal battles.

King felt uncomfortable and isolated from her conservative parents for years, who wouldn't be supportive or understanding of her sexuality; it was only at the age of 51 that King felt comfortable talking about it openly with her parents.

She was an intensely-driven tennis player who was more concerned with personal perfection on the court - "playing the perfect game" - than with competition.

Perhaps due to her sexuality or her drive to be the best, she remained detached in most of her personal relationships, saying "If you want to be the best, you must never let anyone know what you really feel... They can't hurt you if they don't know."

King's most famous accomplishment was winning the "Battle of the Sexes," a highly-publicized male vs. female singles tennis match, in which she soundly defeated former top professional male player Bobby Riggs. This win is still considered an important turning point for women's tennis and for female athletes in general.

Later in her career she successfully led a campaign to make female and male prize winnings equal (women were usually given a significantly smaller purse for winning). In 1973 the US Open Tournament began offering equal prize money as a result of her efforts.

As a tennis player, one of her best-remember qualities was her skill under pressure and her ability to fight back from a losing position to achieve victory. Rosemary Casals, a fellow player, once said "No matter how far down you got her, you could never be sure of beating her."

Between her tennis career and her pivotal social role as a female athlete, she is honored as an incredible player and a crucial force in the advancement of gay rights and feminism.

Jesse Owens (1913-1980)

"The battles that count aren't the ones for gold medals. The struggles within yourself - the invisible, inevitable battles inside all of us - that's where it's at."

"A lifetime of training for just 10 seconds."

Summary:

An African-American track-and-field hero who refused to bow to racial discrimination or oppression in the 50s and 60s... A remarkable, multiple-record-setting athlete who started from nothing, rose to international fame, fell again into poverty and obscurity, and rose once more as an American ambassador of goodwill... A man who became a symbol of the power of the individual to triumph over stereotypes of race and whose life tells a remarkable story of courage and strength!

Vocab word: Bigotry, intolerance or oppression (particularly that based on racism).
Hitler's *bigotry* did not matter when it came time for Owens to dominate the Olympics.

Themes: Courage, the individual vs. society, triumph over adversity, focus, self-discipline, temporary failure, champions and heroes

Facts:

Jesse Owens came from oppressed roots typical of an African-American born near the turn of the century: he was the son of a poor sharecropper, and grandson of a slave.

Owens's world-record performances started at a young age, while he was on his high school track team. The strength of his high school performances led many colleges to try to recruit him; he chose Ohio State.

Ohio State didn't have any track scholarships, so Owens worked multiple jobs to pay for his education, even while studying and continuing his phenomenal athletic career.

As a black man in America in the 1930s, Owens faced daily segregation and discrimination - even when traveling to competitions with his college track team. He had to live off-campus and get take-out food or eat at black-only restaurants.

In 1935, at the Big Ten meet in Ann Arbor, Michigan, he set an incredible three world records and tied a fourth, all within 45 minutes of each other. This is considered one of the greatest athletic achievements of the century by some sports commentators.

In 1936 Owens competed for America at the Summer Olympics in Berlin, Germany. At the time of these Olympics, Hitler was in charge and Nazi power was on the rise in Germany; arrogant declarations of "Aryan supremacy" and the supposed inferiority of blacks were common. Hitler expected his "superior" German athletes to take home most of the Olympic medals.

To the surprise of many (Hitler included), Owens won four gold medals at the Berlin Olympics (100m sprint, 200m sprint, long jump, and relay). Hitler would later explain away this amazing feat as a result "primitive" strength that had an unfair advantage over "civilized" white society.

Not long after the Berlin Olympics, Owens started to have money problems and worked uninspiring jobs in order to live (gas station attendant, dry-cleaner). He was prosecuted for tax evasion, and declared bankruptcy.

When all seemed lost, the U.S. Government appointed him a "goodwill ambassador" and Owens began to return to the spotlight as an inspirational speaker and public relations consultant for private companies. He also maintained strong ties with youth groups and young athletes, as well as with the black community.

In his lifetime, he was presented with the Medal of Freedom, the highest honor for a civilian in the United States. Years after his death, he was also awarded the Medal of Honor.

Muhammad Ali (1942-present)

"I hated every minute of training, but I said, 'Don't quit. Suffer now and live the rest of your life as a champion'."

""You lose nothing when fighting for a cause ... In my mind the losers are those who don't have a cause they care about."

"I am the greatest!"

Summary:

A seemingly-superhuman African American boxer; a master of comically insulting rhymes with which he mocked his opponents; a living symbol of the Civil Rights movement; Muhammad Ali was a champ that fought some of his hardest battles outside the ring.

Vocab word: Fortitude, persistence and courage when faced with pain or adversity.
Ali has shown great *fortitude* both physically and spiritually throughout his life.

Themes: Triumph over adversity, focus, determination, self-discipline, the individual vs. society

Facts:

A descendent of slaves in the American South; he was born under the name "Cassius Clay."

When his bicycle was stolen at the age of 12, he began training in boxing and soon began fighting on a local television show called *Tomorrow's Champions.*

His amateur (unpaid) career was spectacular and he maintained a fight record of 100 wins and only 5 losses. In this time he also won an Olympic gold medal and two national Golden Gloves along with many other boxing awards.

In his autobiography Ali explains that he threw his Olympic Gold Medal into a river after being refused service at a "whites-only" restaurant; his frustration with segregation and discrimination would inform many of his upcoming life decisions.

He began a professional career to a very strong start, going 19-0 from 1960-1963 and defeating some famous and feared opponents along the way.

Ali's fighting style was considered unorthodox for the times; he relied on his quick footwork to avoid punches instead of defending his face with his hands, as most other fighters did, and he was known for his tactic of "rope-a-dope," in which he stayed defensive and allowed his opponent to tire himself out before turning the tables with a flurry of powerful punches. It often worked!

In 1964, "Cassius Clay" announced that he was a member of the Nation of Islam, a group of radical Black Muslims who militantly opposed racism and white oppression. Following in the footsteps of radical black leader Malcolm X, Ali changed his name to "Cassius X" and then to "Muhammad Ali," symbolizing his rebellion against white America and his hope for a separate black nation.

One of Ali's most famous and powerful public statements was his refusal to be drafted into the Vietnam War. He refused on the grounds that the war was opposed to his Islamic religion and also that the war was yet another instance of White oppressors overpowering darker-skinned people. As a conscientious objector, he was arrested and stripped of his titles, but public support for the boxer led to the Supreme Court reversing his conviction.

After he was exonerated, Ali's career as a world-class fighter continued for almost a decade more until his retirement in 1979. After leaving the ring, he took many high-profile leadership positions promoting humanitarian endeavors. It is estimated that he has helped provide more than 22 million meals to feed the hungry across the world!

Ali's legacy as a boxer is as one the absolute greatest of all time - perhaps, even, "the Greatest." Outside the ring, he is known for his refusal to back down on his principles and the great amounts of social activism that he is engaged in. A true champion!

Hamlet by William Shakespeare (written circa 1600)

"There is nothing either good or bad, but thinking makes it so."

"To be, or not to be – that is the question."

Summary:

Shakespeare's classic play, *Hamlet,* is the story of a young prince who must revenge his murdered father, but first must overcome his own guilt and hesitance to act violently. Though the style of speaking may be old-school, the plot is powerful even today – the hesitant young man, the betrayed king, the scheming uncle, the treacherous queen, and the doom they weave for themselves through their own failings. Themes of death, vengeance, and gender relationships run throughout the tale as it builds to a bloody finale.

Vocab word: Vacillating, going back and forth.
Hamlet's famous character flaw lies in his indecision and *vacillation* between right and wrong.

Themes: Acting without complete understanding, revenge, indecision, hesitation

Author's Background:

Shakespeare, an English writer, is of course considered on the most influential and respected authors in history. Primarily a poet and a playwright, he is known for his keen insight into human nature, and his perfectly-structured plots that have been interpreted and reinterpreted in the centuries since his death.

Plot Points:

Hamlet, young prince of Denmark, encounters the ghost of his father, who reveals that he was murdered by Hamlet's uncle Claudius, who successfully schemed to take over the throne and marry Hamlet's mother, Queen Gertrude.

Feigning madness to avoid suspicion, Hamlet begins to plot his revenge on Claudius. However, he has doubts about the reality of his ghostly vision.

Torn between procrastination and action, Hamlet looks for a way to establish Claudius's guilt, which he does by sponsoring a play about murder for the "pleasure" of Claudius. When the murder scene takes place, Claudius leaves the room, which Hamlet takes as a sign of guilt.

During a confrontation with his mother Gertrude, Hamlet kills a royal servant by accident. The man killed turns out to be the father of Ophelia, Hamlet's young lover. She goes mad and drowns herself. Her brother, Laertes, plans violent revenge against Hamlet.

In the dramatic conclusion, nearly every major character, including Hamlet, Claudius, and Gertrude, dies of poison as they kill each other off for various grudges.

Important Symbols:

Yorick's skull – Hamlet moodily contemplates the bones of a court jester that used to entertain him when he was a child. The skull symbolizes the all-powerful, all-consuming nature of death – no one is safe from it, even our childhood friends – and foreshadows the ending of the play, in which essentially everyone ends up dead.

Important Themes:

Indecisiveness and uncertainty – Hamlet craves an impossible certainty that he is morally right to take revenge against Claudius, and this leads to indecisiveness and procrastination. He misses chances to exact revenge until it is too late. This tragic flaw means that although he will successfully avenge his father's death, Hamlet himself will have to die as a result.

Revenge – it seems that every major character wants vengeance on another character for their perceived offenses. The play makes clear the final, disastrous results of seeking "an eye for an eye."

Gender relations – Hamlet finds women weak, distasteful, and untrustworthy. He hates his mother for remarrying Claudius after her husband, Hamlet's father, is murdered. Hamlet also courts Ophelia, but not very seriously, because he doesn't truly respect women. His carelessness with her heart is one of the primary reasons that she ends up killing herself, and again, Hamlet eventually pays the price when Ophelia's brother decides to take revenge on him.

Harry Potter by J.K. Rowling (first published 1997)

"It takes a great deal of bravery to stand up to our enemies, but just as much to stand up to our friends." [Professor Dumbledore, to Harry]

"Dark and difficult times lie ahead. Soon we must all face the choice between what is right and what is easy." [Professor Dumbledore]

Summary:

The story of Harry Potter is an epic tale of a young wizard, and his friends and adventures, which became a worldwide cultural smash hit, much to the surprise (and financial benefit) of the author. The massive, seven-book cycle weaves classic mythology, contemporary culture, and heroic adventure into one very popular young adult's series. If you loved these books and movies and know them like the back of your hand, you can find some great themes and symbols that apply to a wide variety of SAT topics and are fun to use, besides!

Vocab word: Singular, being one-of-a-kind or unique.
Harry displays a *singular* resistance to the powers of the dark lord Voldemort.

Themes: Friendship, leadership, the importance of taking risks, being unique, being gifted, self-sacrifice, the value of education

Author background:

J.K. Rowling was a British woman living on welfare before writing the first Harry Potter novel. The book took off immediately, she wrote six sequels, and within five years she had gone from being quite poor to being a multimillionaire. Today she is one of the wealthiest women in the world, as Harry Potter has been turned into a series of Hollywood blockbuster movies, and toys and games based on the series are now available in every market.

Plot points:

Harry Potter is a young boy that starts off as a nobody, an orphan living with his oppressive relatives, who receives knowledge of his great gifts and destiny in the form of an invitation to attend the Hogwarts School of Witchcraft and Wizardry, a challenge which he gladly accepts.

Harry undergoes a process of development and growth. Through apprenticeships to more experienced mentors, Harry develops his latent magical talents; likewise, through new friendships, he develops leadership skills and begins to find love and acceptance where he previously was abandoned and alone.

Harry has countless adventures and solves many minor mysteries. However, the story moves slowly but unstoppably towards the most important conflict: a confrontation with Lord Voldemort, an exceptionally powerful banished wizard who killed Harry's parents many years ago.

As Voldemort gains power and violence and fear break out among witches and wizards, Harry loses almost everything – his friends, his teachers, his school - and becomes an outcast; all seems lost. He resolves to go on and see his destiny to the end.

Eventually Harry finds his true inner power, and faces and overcomes ultimate evil through the power of love. Voldemort is vanquished and peace returns to the land.

Important Themes:

The Power of Friendship: Harry consistently depends on but also supports his friends. His kindness wins him many allies.

Self-sacrifice: Harry's parents sacrifice their lives to save their child; his most important mentor, Professor Dumbledore, sacrifices himself to protect Harry; Harry himself is willing to sacrifice his own life to save the world from the evil of Lord Voldemort.

The responsibility of special gifts: Wizards and witches are presented in contrast to "Muggles," who are humans without magical powers. Those who can control magic are required to keep themselves hidden from the Muggles. While some "pureblood" wizards hate and scorn Muggles and half-Muggle wizards, others view it as the responsibility of powerful magicians to protect Muggles from dangers that they cannot comprehend.

Good/love is stronger than evil/hate: The ultimate conflict in the *Harry Potter* series. In the end, Harry triumphs because he can depend on his friends to help him, and because of the power of love that Voldemort cannot overcome or understand.

Lord of the Flies, by William Golding (published 1954)

"Kill the pig! Cut his throat! Kill the pig! Bash him in!"

"Ralph wept for the end of innocence, the darkness of man's heart..."

Summary:

The story of a group of schoolboys marooned on an island, the struggles they face to survive, and the failed society they attempt to construct for themselves. Though they make a strong start by electing a leader and making decisions democratically, they begin to lose control of their own violent natures, and their miniature society rapidly tears itself apart, revealing the essential savagery beneath the surface of respectable British civilization.

Vocab word: Degenerate, to disorder or fall apart.
The society of schoolboys constantly threatens to completely *degenerate* into violence and chaos.

Themes: Leadership, the flaws of civilization, the individual vs. society, the power of fear, overcoming hardship, loyalty, overcoming adversity

Author's background:

Golding fought in World War II, which contributed to his somewhat pessimistic view of humanity. More than twenty publishers rejected *Lord of the Flies*, Golding's first novel, before he successfully published it; it went on to be a bestseller, and a common book to study in schools, while Golding would later win a Nobel Prize for his writing.

Plot points:

A group of schoolboys are in a plane crash over the ocean but manage to make it alive to a deserted island. They quickly elect a leader, Ralph, and a rival named Jack appears just as quickly.

Ralph, who takes advice from Piggy (the weakest, most intellectual and most moral of the boys) makes the wise decision to start a signal fire that must be kept burning. The boys use Piggy's glasses as lenses to start the fire, which quickly rages out of control and threatens the island (an early warning of the collapse of civilization that will follow)

Meanwhile, Jack becomes obsessed with hunting, as most of the boys become lazy and unwilling to work to improve their chance at rescue. Ralph becomes more frustrated, Jack gains an increasing amount of power, and Piggy is pushed more and more towards the outside of the group.

The boys begin to fear a "beast" that roams the island; this superstitious terror leads to the murder of Simon, an innocent and friendly boy, who is torn apart by the others when he emerges from the dark forest and startles the others as they dance like savages around a fire.
Finally, Jack gains complete power over the boys and leads them in a manhunt to kill his rival, Ralph.

The boys once again set fire to the island, this time on purpose, in order to kill Ralph at all costs. Just when all seems lost, the boys are rescued by the British Navy, and the boys weep in horror at the realization of what they have become.

Important symbols:

The conch; the glasses – The conch represents democracy and order at first, when at meetings, no boy can speak until he holds the conch. As the boys' tribes degenerate into violence, the conch is smashed when Roger kills Piggy with a boulder. The glasses, which are also destroyed by the boulder, symbolize society, science, logic, reason, and other "refined" and intellectual aspects of humanity – ideals that vanish when men are in a struggle for self-preservation.

"The Lord of the Flies" – as the boys turn to violence and hunt animals for meat, they also become more ritualistic and superstitious. After killing a wild pig, the hunters impale its head on a spike and this terrifying symbol takes hold of the boys' imagination. As the beast itself explains (in a hallucination) to Simon, the impaled head represents the "beast within" each of the boys – the chaotic evil that caused them to abandon law and turn to murder.

Important themes:

Man's "animal nature," which is inherently violent and superstitious; the struggle for power that arises when there are no clear authorities nearby; the struggle for survival and its psychological costs on "civilized" humans; selfish desire vs. compromise for the sake of society.

The Great Gatsby, by F. Scott Fitzgerald (published 1925)

"So we beat on, boats against the current, borne back ceaselessly into the past."

Summary:

A novel about the tangled relationships of old friends and lovers, set in fashionable New York society after World War I. A mysterious man of wealth who holds splendid parties; a beautiful girl and her handsome, violent husband; a former soldier looking to begin a new life as a respectable young man; these are the characters who weave the fatal web of *The Great Gatsby*.

Vocab word: Nouveau riche, the "new rich" or people who acquire their own wealth from nothing. Gatsby is both scorned and respected for being a self-made man, often called the *"Nouveau riche."*

Themes: Self-determination and success, hardship, money doesn't lead to happiness, ethics, loyalty

Author's Background:

An American novelist and story-writer, now considered a symbol of "the Jazz Age," or America in the 1920s. As a representative of this decadent time of cultural revolution, he struggled with alcoholism, and enjoyed luxuries and "the good life," often going into debt to support his habits.

Plot Points:

Our narrator, Nick, has come home from World War I and moved to New York to start a life. He meets up with his socialite cousin Daisy and her "brutish" but handsome husband, Tom, who is secretly having an affair.

Nick, Daisy, and Tom make their way to a high-society party hosted at the mansion of a mysterious man named Gatsby. Gatsby frequently holds lavish parties, but is rarely seen himself.

When Nick finally meets Gatsby, Gatsby reveals that he and Daisy were once in love, but Daisy was wealthy while Gatsby was penniless, and they eventually split up when Gatsby was sent to war. Gatsby never forgot her and came back to earn a fortune in order to impress her.

Daisy and Gatsby are reintroduced and begin their relationship anew, but neither party is as happy as they once were. This unhappiness leads to a confrontation between the main characters, and Tom reveals Gatsby as a criminal whose wealth came from bootlegging alcohol during the Prohibition; Daisy also lacks the strength to leave Tom, though Gatsby was expecting her to come with him. Gatsby has failed in his mission.

On the way home from this confrontation, Daisy hits and kills Tom's mistress while driving Gatsby's car. Gatsby loves her so much that he takes the blame, and he is murdered several days later by the husband of Tom's mistress. Nick, the narrator, learns that Tom was involved in the murder, and decides to leave this corrupt society for good.

Important Symbols:

"The Green Light" – a famous and mystical symbol from this novel; Gatsby can see the light of Daisy's boat dock from the distance of his own home. It has been interpreted many ways – as a symbol of romantic longing, as the obsessive pursuit of "green" money, as the "green" of jealousy, as the green traffic light that means "go."

The eyes of Doctor Eckelburg – Nick sees a faded billboard with a pair of eyes staring out over the landscape. Their symbolism is never made clear, but many readers have interpreted them as the eyes of God, judging the failures of American society.

Important Themes:

As a commentary on contemporary American culture of the time, *The Great Gatsby* reveals the shallowness of idolizing wealth and glamour, and reveals the dark side of the wild parties and revelry that concealed a deep national unhappiness and restlessness following World War I.

The novel demonstrates how we can idolize people and things that don't deserve our worship, such as money, which ultimately proves useless as a way for Gatsby or Nick to find love or happiness. Gatsby's infatuation with Daisy, who proves unworthy of his love because of her shallow, inconsistent nature, is a second example of expecting too much personal fulfillment from an outside person or possession.

The American Great Depression (1929-1930s)

"It came with a speed and ferocity that left men dazed. The bottom simply fell out of the market.....
The streets were crammed with a mixed crowd - agonized little speculators... sold-out traders...
inquisitive individuals and tourists seeking a closer view of the national catastrophe..... Where was
it going to end?" [The New York Times, reporting on the 1929 stock market crash]

"One woman said she borrowed 50 cents from a friend and bought stale bread for 3 cents per loaf,
and that is all they had for 11 days except for one or two meals.... Another family did not food for
two days. Then the husband went out and gathered dandelions and the family lived on them [as
food]."

Summary:

The Great Depression was a time of great suffering and poverty across much of the
industrialized world in the late 1920s and into the 1930s. In America, luxuries were scarce, jobs were
almost impossible to find, and families were under severe strain just to put food on the table.
Eventually, the government created enough projects to employ workers to improve America's public
spaces and roads, and the economy slowly recovered. The Depression is often used as a parable for the
consequences of greed and careless speculation in the stock market.

Vocab word: Nadir, the low point of something.
The Great Depression represents the all-time *nadir* of the American economy.

Themes: Triumph over adversity, hardship, greed, leadership, cycles of good and bad

Facts:

An economic "depression" is an unfortunate period of time marked by high unemployment, high
bankruptcy rates, less industrial production, less money available to borrow, inflation of currency, etc.
Standards of living typically become lower for large groups of the population.

The American Great Depression began in the US on "Black Tuesday" in October 1929, when the stock
prices of major American companies fell suddenly and dramatically. The worldwide economy felt the
catastrophic effects soon afterwards and other countries suffered similar depressions.

After the stock crash, many people lost their savings and investments and became reluctant to spend
any more than necessary to survive. As a result, companies had fewer people buying their products,

and the Depression dragged on as industry couldn't pull itself out without buyers.

In 1930, the American government tried to protect American companies by heavily taxing imported goods, a tariff that was intended to increase American profits. Instead, foreign countries vengefully did the same thing to America, and foreign markets for American goods dried up, actually making the situation worse.

"It never rains, but it pours" - ironically, a severe drought hit America's farmlands in 1930, causing a scarcity of food, and further economic problems as farmers couldn't turn a profit and sold their farms. Government intervention was felt necessary to confront such an enormous national problem.

President Franklin D. Roosevelt contributed to the eventual recovery through his "New Deal" program. One of the central features of the New Deal was creating government-funded jobs for the unemployed through the CCC (Civilian Conservation Corps) and WPA (Work Projects Administration), which used the new labor force to build roads, public buildings, and other projects which would benefit the country as a whole.

Although these programs helped turn the economy around, many scholars view America's entry into World War II as the end of the Great Depression. In wartime, production increased and previously-jobless men and women found employment as soldiers and assembly-line workers.

Explanations for the Great Depression, and theories about how to prevent another one, are still topics of intense discussion among economists; the reality is that many different causes contributed to the problem.

Although we may always fear the specter of another Great Depression, economists have since come to understand high and low points in the economy as naturally-occurring, healthy cycles.

World War I (1914-1918)

""Two armies that fight each other are like one large army that commits suicide." [Henri Barbusse, a French soldier in World War I]

""This is not a peace. It is an armistice [temporary cease-fire] for twenty years." [Ferdinand Foch, a French general, commenting on the terms of the Treaty of Versailles that ended the war. He was proved correct when World War II began twenty years later]

Summary:

World War I has been seen as a cataclysmic event that shook humanity's faith in its own basic decency, a global loss of innocence. The combination of lethal and untested advanced weaponry with 200-year-old battlefield tactics and dated conceptions of "honorable" warfare led to one pointless slaughter after another. Even the peace that followed was a disaster: the victors of World War I imposed such harsh terms on the losers that tensions boiled over twenty years later in the even more violent Second World War.

Vocab word: Cataclysmic, being completely destructive and disastrous, as a natural disaster. The new artillery and weapons of World War I lead to *cataclysmic* battles.

Themes: Following authority, the dark side of technology and innovation, the dark side of loyalty (between countries that were dragged into the war by old alliances), connection of art and society

Facts:

Background tension to the war was caused by the desire of powerful European nations to continually expand their territory and claim and control more resources and land.

The outbreak of actual hostilities was triggered by the assassination of Archduke Franz Ferdinand of Austria; this led to war between Austria-Hungary and Serbia, and old treaties quickly drew other, more powerful nations into the war.

War technology had recently made significant advances in recent years, and murderous weapons such as the machine gun, heavy artillery, and horrific poisonous gasses were deployed for the first time in large-scale warfare.

Fighting tactics lagged behind the advanced military technology, and commanders assaulting heavily-defending positions would send literally tens or hundreds of thousands of soldiers to their deaths as they charged into the mechanized hail of bullets. World War I eventually claimed the lives of over 9 million combatants.

The war finally ended with the Treaty of Versailles, which forced Germany to accept responsibility for the war, and make massive economic reparations (or repayments) to the victors. The harsh terms of the treaty were designed to prevent Germany from ever making war on Europe again, but they turned out to be extremely counterproductive.

The losers of World War I (specifically, Germany) were punished so harshly by the victorious nations that they suffered severe economic and social problems after the war. This would later facilitate Hitler's rise to power as the German people sought an explanation for their unhappiness and an outlet for their frustrations.

World War I decimated continental Europe while sparing the United States across the ocean; this led directly to the establishment of the U.S. as a world superpower.

The effects of World War I on society were immediate and far-reaching. The war can be seen as a kind of international "loss of innocence" – an unbelievable amount of men were sent to their deaths, and survivors came back changed forever by the memories of the horrors they had witnessed.

Similarly, the arts and music took a dark turn as the rage, sadness, and violence of the war found expression through creative channels. World civilization as it was known had been profoundly and permanently altered by the vast scope of violence.

The end results of World War I are also agreed to be root causes of World War II only two decades later. European nations became more "nationalistic" and felt themselves naturally superior to other nations, leading to an international culture of suspicion and distrust. Hitler's Nazi Germany would eventually become the most famous example of this violent nationalism.

The Wright Brothers (Turn of the 19th century)

"The desire to fly is an idea handed down to us by our ancestors who, in their grueling travels across trackless lands in prehistoric times, looked enviously on the birds soaring freely through space, at full speed, above all obstacles, on the infinite highway of the air." [Orville Wright]

"The Wright Brothers created the single greatest cultural force since the invention of writing. The airplane became the first World Wide Web, bringing people, languages, ideas, and values together." [Bill Gates]

Summary:

Two of the most famous inventors of all time, Orville and Wilbur Wright are remembered as the first humans to tame the skies with powered, heavier-than-air flight. The great personal and financial risks they took, along with the doubts they surely overcame, define them as a dynamic team that always backed up their creative thought with direct application.

Vocab word: Tenacious, never giving up, stubborn.
Even when their funds ran low, the Wright Brothers showed a tenacious persistence in their research.

Themes: Technological innovation, persistence, risk-taking, teamwork, individuals vs. society

Facts:

Orville and Wilbur were two of seven children born to a family in the Midwest United States. Later in life, they pointed to a toy "helicopter" that their father brought them as an inspiration for their fascination with flight.

Both brothers attended high school, but neither attended diplomas.

Wilbur was hit in the face during an ice-hockey game and lost his front teeth; this injury affected his personality and he didn't attend college as he had planned. Wilbur himself would express concern over his own lack of ambition.

The brothers went into business together as bicycle repairmen, observing the opportunity presented by the rising craze for the bicycle as a means of transportation.

Just before the turn of the 19th century, important breakthroughs in human flight were happening across the world; humanity seemed on the brink of heavier-than-air flight. In 1896, one man, Otto Lilienthal, even died testing a glider aircraft.

Orville and Wilbur began experimenting with flying machines around this time, basing their work and designs on previous theorists and inventors such as Leonardo da Vinci, and Lilienthal (the man that died in 1896 testing his own glider).

One of the brothers' most important sources of information and data, however, was not from humans, but from careful observation of birds and the methods they used to take to the air and control their flight.

At this time in history, flight presented not only the difficulty of how to get *into* the air and stay there, but also the question of how to control a flying machine once aloft. Preferring not to reinvent the wheel, Orville and Wilbur studied the question of flight from the point of view of Nature, which had already solved this problem.

The brothers spent several years testing designs at the now-famous Kitty Hawk beach site and refined their glider designs until they developed an effective unpowered flyer in 1902. Soon afterwards they added power in the form of a propeller, although the machine required so much expertise to control that only Orville or Wilbur themselves could control the plane.

Even for the next several years, the public and the press could be skeptical of their accomplishments - one headline read "FLYERS OR LIARS?" The brothers were so ahead of their times that their successes were too amazing to be believed by many.

Their designs were quickly copied and larger-scale businesses began to turn profits from their innovations, which resulted in a long-term patent war to control the intellectual property of heavier-than-air flight. The brothers won, although ironically this led to them being somewhat villianized for profiteering, despite the fact that they had previously been viewed as heroes.

Despite this difficulty during their lifetime, their shared legacy is one of near-universal admiration by pilots, aircraft designers, and inventors around the world. In their willingness to take risks in the pursuit of remarkable opportunity, and their ingenuity in responding to one of the oldest human desires of flight, they earned their place in the halls of history.

Bernard "Bernie" Madoff (1938-present)

"Mr. Madoff's crimes were extraordinarily evil." [US District Judge Denny Chin]

"*$@# my victims. I carried them for twenty years, and now I'm doing 150 years." [Madoff, to a fellow prison inmate who expressed sympathy for those that Madoff swindled]

Summary:

"Bernie" Madoff pulled off what was probably the greatest con of all time and robbed rich and poor, young and old alike through his fake Wall Street investment firm. A seemingly remorseless and evil financial genius, he has shown little concern for his victims, most of who will never see a cent of their life savings. His case became a symbol of corruption in the American financial industry in a recession as the nation searched for a scapegoat to blame their woes on and he was sentenced to a symbolic 150-year prison sentence at the age of 70.

Vocab word: Charlatan, a fraud, fake, or swindler.
Bernie Madoff will go down in history as one of the greatest *charlatans* of all time.

Themes: Money does not lead to happiness, risk-taking, immoral behavior, the flaws of our heroes, people believe what they want to believe, greed

Facts:

Born in New York City, he was a third-generation immigrant and came from a modest family background. After attending college, he founded his own Wall Street investment firm at a young age, which he controlled for 48 years.

Through connections and family ties, Madoff ensured that his firm continued to grow and it became an extremely large and powerful firm controlling billions of dollars of other people's investment money.

Madoff managed the public image of his firm to make it seem very desirable and exclusive - even to the point of turning down money from some who wanted to invest. Calculated moves such as this increased the demand for his services and made him well-known among wealthy investors.

The investment returns that Madoff claimed for his firm were staggeringly high, even suspicious, but starry-eyed investors chasing easy money learned not to ask questions and simply provided Madoff's company with more and more money.

Experts and other investment companies remained suspicious of Madoff's unrealistic claims, but the SEC, a government commission responsible for overseeing investment activity, never looked closely enough at Madoff's firm to discover the massive Ponzi (or "pyramid") scam that he maintained successfully for decades.

Madoff's corrupt business practices earned him hundreds of millions of dollars; he lived a life of absolute luxury, buying houses across the world, collecting expensive watches and shoes, affecting national politics through his social and financial influence, and buying boats and private jets.

In 2008, amid allegations of wrongdoing (one frustrated financial analyst spent almost a decade trying to convince the world that Madoff was operating illegally), Madoff admitted to his sons that his business was based entirely on fraud. His sons reported him to the authorities and Madoff was successfully prosecuted and imprisoned, his assets confiscated.

The judge sentenced Madoff, an elderly man, to the maximum sentence of 150 years, for the "extraordinary evil" and harm that the large-scale fraud had caused the people of the United States.

It wasn't just the very wealthy that lost their money in Madoff's giant fraud (the largest financial scam in history) - unremarkable, middle-class families also lost their entire life savings in a matter of minutes; many lives have been ruined, because the money is simply "no longer there" - most small investors will never see their money again and have nowhere to turn.

One of Madoff's sons, Mark, (who was involved in the family business) committed suicide exactly two years after his father's arrest - it is difficult not to see the suicide as connected to a vast shame over his father's illegal acts, and potentially over his own guilt as well - it is unclear exactly how involved Madoff's family was, as he refused to provide such information at his trial.

Madoff's legacy is as an unrepentant sociopath who robbed thousands of innocent people to live a life of ease and comfort. Though he has lost everything he once had, he still seems proud of his "accomplishment" and the fact that he will go down in history as one of the greatest con artists of all time. His story also raises an uncomfortable issue: that many of his investors may have been deluding themselves out of greed for "easy money." Bernie Madoff will be certainly be an American moral parable for generations to come.

Henry Ford (1863-1947)

"It has been my observation that most people get ahead during the time that others waste."

"Nothing is particularly hard if you divide it into small jobs."

Summary:

Henry Ford is remembered as one of the most successful businessmen and engineers of all time; his automobiles sparked a revolution in personal travel and made Ford a vast fortune. It was not only his cars that earned him his fame, but his production methods as well – his massive factories proved the effectiveness of assembly-line-style production over making products by hand. Ford is also remembered as a good-hearted and generous man who took care of his workers like family, and was a model industrialist in a time when many tycoons exploited their power.

Vocab word: Tycoon, an exceptionally successful businessperson.
Ford's success as a *tycoon* of the automobile industry spoke to his hard work and inventiveness.

Themes: Leadership, self-made success, innovation, technology, teamwork, goal-setting, hard work

Facts:

Ford was born on a farm near Detroit, but hated farm life and left home to work as a lowly apprentice machinist after his mother died.

At a young age he demonstrated an excellent grasp of technology by taking apart and putting back together pocket watches, and operating and servicing steam engines.

In his late 20s, Ford was employed as Chief Engineer with the Edison Illuminating Company. This helped financially support his experiments with gas-powered engines and vehicles.

After an encouraging meeting with the legendary inventor Thomas Edison himself, Ford renewed his work on a four-wheeled, gas-powered personal vehicle. Development continued, and Ford founded several automobile companies, although he encountered financial difficulties as his manufacturing method and automobile design were not yet perfected.

1908 saw the introduction of Ford's "Model T" car, which was simple to manufacture, drive, and repair. Ford learned how to publicize his invention and gained a great deal of attention in the press and through advertising. As his cars became widely available, American motor culture sprouted across the country in the form of car clubs, races, and personal vehicle ownership for those other than the super-rich.

It's not just for his car and his wealth that Ford is famous - his factories pioneered the assembly-line construction method, in a search for efficiency, and production skyrocketed. The basic Ford production model is still copied and adapted by manufacturing companies to this day.

Though it is popularly believed that Ford came up with his inventive ideas alone, there is more credible evidence that he asked intelligent questions of his specialized advisors and listened to his employees in order to further refine his methods, rather than futilely trying to do everything himself.

One of Ford's greatest legacies is as a businessman and industrialist who refused to exploit his workers for his own gain - he voluntarily paid his workers far more than the average of the day, and attracted the best and brightest employees as a result.

Ford was a deeply moral man. He was an avowed pacifist who opposed war as a horrendous waste of lives, money, and technology. He believed in human dignity and for a time, informally required "good behavior" and temperance from his employees - no gambling, heavy drinking, etc.

Ford is remembered as an industrial pioneer and one of the most successful self-made businesspeople in history. Though he invented neither the automobile nor the assembly line himself, it was his legendary Ford Motor Company that demonstrated the possibilities of both vehicle and production plant. Despite his great wealth, Ford never lost touch with the common American and kept his high-minded ideals central to his work and legacy. His determination, hard work, creativity, and success will forever mark him as one of the most "American" of American historical figures.

Malcolm X (1925-1965)

"I believe in the brotherhood of all men, but I don't believe in wasting brotherhood on anyone who doesn't want to practice it with me. Brotherhood is a two-way street."

"Be peaceful, be courteous, obey the law, respect everyone; but if someone puts his hand on you, send him to the cemetery."

Summary:

Malcolm X was a militant black leader in the 50s and 60s, an advocate for violent change who was seen as a counterweight to the more peaceful Martin Luther King, Jr. Malcolm's young life was filled with violence, crime, and drugs; after a transformative prison sentence, he converted to Islam and used his ferocious powers of oratory to unite blacks and frighten the white establishment. He never backed down, even though he knew how many dangerous enemies he was making, and even predicted his own assassination, which occurred as he spoke in New York City.

Vocabulary word: Subversive, a person who tries to overthrow an established government.
Malcom X was feared as a potentially dangerous *subversive* by some powerful white people of his era.

Themes: Leadership, violence as a source of change, personal transformation, triumph over adversity

Facts:

Malcolm X was born "Malcolm Little" in the mid-'20s in the United States and saw firsthand the dangers of being African-American in a racist, segregated society: KKK threats led his parents to relocate from their home.

While still a boy, Malcolm's father was hit and killed by a streetcar (accounts disagree about whether it was an accident, a murder, or a suicide) and his mother suffered a nervous breakdown, so Malcolm and his siblings were sent to separate foster homes.

Malcolm was one of the best students in his school, but he dropped out when a teacher told him that his dream of being a lawyer was not a realistic goal for a black man. Instead, he moved to Harlem and became seriously involved in drug dealing, robbery, and other forms of crime. Eventually he was caught, arrested, and sent to prison.

While in prison, Malcolm experienced a major transformation - he met an inmate who commanded "total respect...with words," and desired to learn how to control such a power. He began to educate himself, reading the books in the prison library, and learned of the teachings of the Nation of Islam, which would profoundly affect the course of his life.

The Nation of Islam envisioned a new nation of blacks - those living in Africa, and those that were separated in America by the slave trade; the Nation preached that white people were "devils," a belief that Malcolm sympathized with, as he could not remember a single white person in his life that had not mistreated or exploited him.

Before leaving prison, Malcolm replaced his last name with the symbol "X" to symbolize the long-lost family name of his African ancestors; in his view, his previous last name, "Little," was representative of slavemasters and had been forced upon him.

Now educated, hardened by prison, and in service to his new political and religious ideals, Malcolm quickly built a large and devoted following of blacks and became a nationally-recognized figure with an alarming (to the white "ruling class) degree of influence.

As the Civil Rights movement gathered strength, Malcolm X was frequently seen as an alternate voice to Martin Luther King, Jr. Where King preached nonviolence and patience, Malcolm advocated for violence, rebellion, and immediate action.

In 1964, Malcolm X, feeling limited and betrayed by the Nation of Islam's leadership, formed his own independent organization for black Americans. He made the traditional Islamic pilgrimage to Mecca, and returned a changed man who believed nonviolence might be the best way to proceed with his goals. This earned the anger of the Nation of Islam, who Malcolm now indirectly opposed.

In February of 1965, Malcolm X was assassinated as he made a speech in New York City. Although the responsible party has never been clearly identified, both the Nation of Islam and the American government have been blamed for the killing. Though he was a controversial figure among the black community, many worldwide mourned his passing, including Martin Luther King, Jr.

Malcolm X left a multi-faceted legacy: he brought hope and self-esteem to many oppressed black Americans, who heard in his rage-filled speeches a reflection of their own frustrations and indignities. He frightened the establishment and fearlessly risked (and eventually, gave) his life for his cause.

Although he is remembered primarily for advocating violence in the fight for civil rights, his eventual conversion to less-violent methods showed a man always willing to reexamine his own beliefs, committed to helping the oppressed in whatever way was most effective.

Florence Nightingale (1820-1910)

"The very first requirement in a hospital is that it should do the sick no harm."

"Nursing is an art, and if it is to be made an art, it requires an exclusive devotion as hard a preparation, as any painter's or sculptor's work; for what is the having to do with dead canvas or dead marble, compared with having to do with the living body?"

Summary:

Florence Nightingale was a founding figure in the world of nursing; she was a kindhearted healer and a soothing presence who became the archetypal representation of the soft-hearted but strong-willed nurse, and her writings paved the way for nursing as a legitimate profession. Her determination advanced not only medicine, but the cause of feminism as well.

Vocab word: Empathetic, showing a deep understanding of other's physical and emotional feelings. Florence Nightingale's success as a healer was partially based on her ability to be *empathetic*.

Themes: Compassion, innovation, focus and determination, the power of the individual

Facts:

Florence was born to a rich, upper-class British family.

At only 17 she believed she was called by God to become a nurse and worked hard to educate herself in this subject despite the serious objections of her family, who expected her to follow the conventional path of being a wife and mother. She even rejected a well-connected suitor's offer of marriage in order to focus on her calling!

In the early 1850s, the large-scale Crimean War broke out in Europe and Nightingale organized a staff of women volunteers (who she helped train herself) to help the British wounded.

This wartime experience taught her volumes about practical care for the wounded (such as the importance of sanitary conditions).

Among the soldiers, she was known as "The Lady with the Lamp" and was beloved by many for her gentle, sympathetic nature. The nickname came from her habit of staying awake to care for the wounded long into the night after everyone else had gone to sleep.

Because of her emerging celebrity after the Crimean War, she was able to raise funds from the public to train more nurses. She wrote the short book *Notes on Nursing*, published in 1859, which further legitimized nursing as a profession.

Her efforts also eventually reformed health care in British poor-houses. Previously, the poor were cared for by nobody except other, healthier poor residents. Nightingale introduced professional nurses into the houses, which paved the way for more public health care measures in the long-term.

One of Nightingale's most influential students, Linda Richards, became a vital force in the nursing profession in the United States.

Although Nightingale was unimpressed with the women of her time in general, she is seen as an important personality in the early feminist movement, because of the inner strength she displayed in rebelling against accepted female roles in her society.

Her legacies are numerous - as a strong-willed, independent woman; as a medical and public-health pioneer; as a member of the first wave of professional female nurses. Her name and personality have become symbolic of compassionate care and healing.

Hippocrates (460 BC - 370 BC)

"Cure sometimes, treat often, comfort always."

"There are in fact two things, science and opinion; the former begets knowledge, the latter ignorance."

Summary:

Hippocrates is a critical figure in the history of medicine; his methods and attitudes towards sickness and patient care improved the standards of medicine as his followers adopted his ideas. Before Hippocrates, medicine was not an independent profession and was often practiced by barbers or mystical healers. In contrast, Hippocrates approached medicine almost like a philosopher, or scientist. His new views upset many traditions, and he once spent 20 years in prison for opposing accepted authority.

Vocab word: Iconoclast, someone who destroys old ways of thinking.
Hippocrates was an *iconoclast* in the field of early medicine and healing.

Themes: Innovation, compassion, leadership, the individual vs. society, organizing/categorizing

Facts:

Considered "the father of western medicine."

An ancient Greek physician that led a medical revolution resulting in medicine becoming a separate and independent profession.

Was imprisoned for twenty years after publicly opposing current medical "wisdom."

He came from a fairly wealthy family; he learned medicine from his father (also a physician) and grandfather and studied a wide variety of subjects from a young age.

Practiced medicine his whole life and traveled fairly widely.

Is credited as the first person to realize that disease had natural, not superstitious or supernatural, causes.

Separated medicine and religion where they were previously linked (e.g. he argued that sickness was not a punishment from the gods).

Pointed to environmental factors, diet, and lifestyle as more important causes of good or ill health; he believed in the importance of "whole-body" health, rather than focusing narrowly on individual parts of the body.

Promoted a kind, caring, and "natural" style of medical treatment that emphasized the body's natural healing processes.

Put a new emphasis on medical professionalism, including staying honest, calm, and serious with patients.

Heavily emphasized the ethical responsibilities of physicians and created a code of ethics that is still used as a model for medical and other professions to this day.

Developed and taught methods of observation and note-taking in order to help future doctors and patients treat similar illnesses.

His teachings were so revered that after his death, nobody expected to be able to improve upon them, and medical advancement saw very little progress for some time.

His legacy is as a wise, dignified, observant and extremely intelligent man of medicine, who single-handedly advanced his field significantly. He has been called "the ideal physician."

He is remembered both as a practical healer and a legendary teacher who perfectly balanced real-life practice and idealistic theory.

Personal Experience: Learning to play the piano

"The piano is able to communicate the subtlest universal truths by means of wood, metal and vibrating air."
Kenneth Miller

"Without music life would be a mistake."
Friedrich Nietzsche

Summary:

My relationship with the piano has been a rocky one, starting with my forced practice in 2nd grade and culminating in personal victory when I took first place in a prestigious competition as a senior in college. Along the way I've learned lessons about patience, perseverance, and personal development; the piano has been a way to learn about myself and the world. It quite literally has changed my life forever.

Vocab word: Eschew, to shun, reject, or abstain from.
While many of my classmates partied every night, I *eschewed* drinking in favor of practicing the piano.

Themes: Persistence, self-determination and success, facing your fears

Facts:

I started taking piano lessons in 2nd grade because my mother told me I had to. I didn't want to go to my first lesson, and I didn't enjoy doing my weekly practice. I found the piano boring and difficult. Years went by without any enjoyment; I simply practiced because my parents would punish me if I didn't.

As a boy, I feared recitals and public performances; I was terrified of making a mistake and being judged or laughed at by the audience, my teachers, or my family.

It's no surprise that I eventually dropped my piano lessons for a couple of years once I had some "say" in the decision. But later, I developed an interest in video game theme songs and, because I knew just enough about music, I was able to play them on the piano. Finally was making my own decisions about music instead of just following orders from my parents and teachers.

I began to seek hidden pianos in out-of-the-way spots, like the abandoned chapel at my summer camp, to practice and play free from the judgments of others (most of whom, I began to realize, don't even play music themselves and take no risks).

In high school my interest in music started to grow on its own as I was good enough to play keyboard and guitar in a rock band with my friends. I started taking the piano more seriously and practiced daily of my own free choice.

Still, because of my inconsistency and lack of commitment, when I got to college, I was one of the worst pianists in the music department. However, my interest in classical music had grown so deep that I was spending hours each day listening to recordings of great professional pianists... and I was learning and practicing what I heard.

While other, more gifted, students would practice for 30 minutes and then go party, I would spend hours in the practice room in deep concentration. Some days I would spend over six hours practicing, and although it was incredibly exhausting work, I now loved every minute of it. I couldn't tear myself away!

Despite (in fact, *because of*) my long-held fear of performing, I put myself out of my comfort zone and played solo recitals, as well as organizing and leading chamber music groups to play my favorite music. Slowly I transformed my reputation from the weakest pianist in the music building to one of the top students in the department.

By the time I was a senior, I had played over a dozen recitals, won multiple awards, and took first place in the most prestigious on-campus music competition. Looking back, music, and the piano, was motivations that forced me to develop persistence, dedication, grace under pressure, self-discipline, and leadership abilities.

Now, music is one of the most important things in my life, and I play many instruments and practice every day - except practice isn't work anymore, it's pure play! Music is a way to let off steam, express myself, make friends happy, and find new goals to chase.

I see now that my musical and personal development always went hand-in-hand; when I was uncommitted and unfocused, that was when I could barely play. As I developed discipline and work ethic, and found my own motivations to succeed, my abilities skyrocketed and my self-respect grew.

Personal Experience: Traveling Abroad

"The world is a book and those who do not travel read only one page." [St. Augustine]

"Not all those who wander are lost." [J.R.R. Tolkien]

Summary:

Travel has always been regarded as a kind of "second education," a real-world counterpart to book study and math problems. In my own experience, there is nothing like travel to amaze you, scare you, stress you out, and ultimately blow your mind. Setting off on your own or with your friends can be a great source of SAT essay evidence – think about the ways you grew and changed, how you rethought (specific) previous assumptions, and give lots of details about what happened to you and what you saw!

Vocab Word: Peregrinations, travels from one place to another, journeys.
I feel that I learned more from a month of *peregrinations* than I did from four years in school.

Themes: The importance of different viewpoints, freedom and independence, risk-taking

Facts:

My parents both worked for Delta Airlines; both were frequently gone for days at a time. Because of this early initiation, I've always thought of travel, and being far from home, as a natural part of life.

My earliest memory is of seeing the Eiffel Tower all lit up at night, my dad and I walking to it late at night as my mom slept in the hotel. This romantic image has always inspired my wanderlust - an atmosphere of mystery and excitement always accompanies my travels: who will I meet? What will I see?

An 8th grade school trip to England and Scotland was my first taste of real freedom in another country; free from my parents' watchful eyes, I bought a sword, wandered the streets, ate where I pleased, and held hands with my first "girlfriend." It was something about the freedom inspired me to be more outgoing and overcome my shyness around girls that I liked - just one of many ways that travel has helped me grow.

For a semester in college, I studied abroad in Edinburgh, Scotland - the land of my ancestors. I remember taking walks in the early morning through the cobbled streets, over the hills. I visited ruins of castles, skipped rocks from the shores of frigid lakes, tasted haggis, and liked it (if you don't know what "haggis" is, look it up!)

I stopped in Vienna, Austria, where I visited the grave of my hero, Beethoven. In the midst of Christmas snows, I walked the same streets and hallways that the great classical musicians lived in, I felt my connection to history, and developed a better understanding of the music that I was studying at the time.

In Florence, Italy, I saw the famous beauty of their cathedral, paid my respects to the sculptures of Michelangelo, and, as homesickness set in, I found a garden that reminded me of home and watched the sun set and dreamt of being among my own family again.

Among all this, I learned the difficulty of being so far from home, for so long. Eventually, the accents lose their charm, the new foods seem bland. When you're in another country, you never truly belong or fit in. Yet you can always find a new friend who will take you by the hand and guide you to new adventures or take you in for a meal.

When I came home, my own land seemed foreign. I related a little less to the stereotypical, close-minded American that never thought of the world outside their own borders. The cheap, tasteless fast-food restaurants looked ugly and unhealthy. Our hodgepodge of popular culture felt almost embarrassing; the noisy commercials for large vehicles were garish and unrefined. I felt out of place at home.

The readjustment period took some time. Eventually I remembered all the good things about my home country, saw my friends and family again, and stopped focusing so much on how America didn't measure up to the new places I had seen. Over the months and years, my travel experiences integrate themselves into my life and rearrange my perspective. They are always experiences of growth, challenge, and learning.

So what do I love about travel? That's a tough question to pin down... it's the sights, the sounds, the new foods. It's the different styles of architecture, the different languages that charm my ears. The difficulties that must be overcome - road signs I can't understand, maps I can't read, hotels I can't find. I love the back alleys, the unexpected detours, the unplanned day you spend in a small town because you weren't precisely on time and your train connection pulled out of the station in front of your eyes. I love the stories, the photographs, the journal entries. I'm in it for the memories, and I'm never disappointed.

Charles Darwin (1809-1882)

"It's not the strongest of the species that survive, nor the most intelligent, but the one responsive to change."

"I am turned into a sort of machine for observing facts and grinding out conclusions."

Summary:

Charles Darwin is a Promethean figure in Western science. His Theory of Natural Selection, otherwise known as the theory of evolution, rewrote society's view of its own place in the cosmos and launched entire new branches of science. The concept of "evolution" has since found useful applications in fields from astronomy to poetry. Darwin has become symbolic of the brilliance of human observational powers and scientific thought.

Vocab word: Contravene, to conflict with.
Darwin's findings directly *contravened* the commonly-accepted religious doctrines of his day.

Themes: Breaking with tradition, observation and knowledge, innovation, the power of the individual

Facts:

An English naturalist whose pioneering theories about evolution and natural selection revolutionized both science and popular culture

He was born to a wealthy family in England; his father was a doctor, and Charles's education was originally directed towards medical study.

Even from a young age, Charles enjoyed collecting and categorizing, skills that would be crucial for his later scientific accomplishments.

Darwin found medicine uninteresting but developed an interest in natural history and marine biology. This led to him becoming a "gentleman observer" on a famous five-year journey of a ship known as the "HMS Beagle."

The variety of human cultures, geological formations, and especially animal life that he saw on this voyage led Darwin to consider the idea that species of animals could change their characteristics over time to fit their environment; that "one species does change into another."

Years of research, study, and theorizing eventually led to the publishing of his legendary book *On the Origin of Species* in 1859.

In this internationally-popular book, Darwin put forth his theory of natural selection - that any small, random variation that gave an individual creature a minor advantage in its environment would have a better chance at surviving and being passed down to the next generation.

Public response was immediate and controversial - the subject was considered a battleground between religion and science, and to many people, Darwin's theories represented a triumph of science over religion.

Even after his death, Darwin has been seen as a champion of rational thought and scientific inquiry; a researcher unafraid afraid of upsetting conventional beliefs in his hunt for the truth.

The controversial questions that he raised about man's descent from apes and ape-like ancestors have forced humans to reexamine their place in the cosmos and have remained relevant for over a hundred years.

Jane Goodall (1934 - present)

"Anyone who tries to improve the lives of animals invariably comes in for criticism from those who believe such efforts are misplaced in a world of suffering humanity."

"I wanted to talk to the animals like Dr. Doolittle!"

Summary:

Jane Goodall is a singular woman who "conquered" the wild by befriending it. She is the first and only human being to be accepted into a wild chimpanzee troop, and her observations and compassionate scientific research are considered groundbreaking. After rising to fame as the woman who lived in the wild with chimps, she has used her celebrity to protect and defend wild and captive animals, and is an advocate for vegetarianism.

Vocab word: Preternatural, differing from or surpassing the natural.
Goodall's ability to bond with wild primates seems almost *preternatural*.

Themes: Following your passion, empathy, risk-taking, adventure

Facts:

As a child, she was given a toy chimpanzee that started her love of animals at a young age

When she was a young woman, she took uninspiring jobs for several years before contacting Louis Leakey, a prominent archeologist, to talk about animals; one thing led to another, and before she knew it Goodall had been recruited to study chimpanzees in the wild.

At the age of only 26, Goodall, who had little formal training, began living in the wild with chimpanzees in Gombe National Park in Africa.

Her patience and determination allowed her to accomplish what no researcher before her could do - she gradually moved closer and closer to them over the course of months until they trusted her and she could sit among them. To this day, she is the only human being that has been fully accepted into a wild chimpanzee society (ironically, the chimps considered her the lowest-ranking member of their tribe!)

"Common knowledge" of the era before Goodall was that chimps were violent, simple beasts. She turned this on her head with revolutionary observations of tool use, organized social structure, and individual personalities.

Although it must have been hard for her to accept, after she formed an emotional bond with the chimps that she studied, Goodall also began to witness a darker side to chimpanzee behavior - she witnessed a "war" between two different groups of chimps and saw adult chimps mercilessly killing infants of their own species. However, because of her honesty and scientific integrity, she continued to honestly report what she observed.

In 1975, African rebels kidnapped four research assistants from Goodall's facility, and most American and European researchers left the area for their own safety - Goodall, however, chose to remain to conduct her research.

Her research in Africa lasted two decades, and her work with chimpanzees has been life-long. Since concluding her direct observations, she has used her fame to improve treatment of chimps in laboratories and zoos, and to protect natural chimpanzee habitats. She is also a committed vegetarian who speaks out against factory farms and the industrial production of meat.

Naturally, such a high-profile figure has often attracted controversy in the scientific community - Goodall has had to address concerns that she abandoned objectivity due to her emotional attachment to her chimp subjects. However, her research is considered indispensable and impressive by the majority of her peers.

Goodall's legacy is as a devoted, determined woman scientist who broke new ground in a difficult field. She will be remembered not only as a scientist, but as a compassionate activist for the causes she believed in.

Marie Curie (1867 - 1934)

"Nothing in life is to be feared. It is only to be understood."

"I have no dress except the one I wear every day. If you are going to be kind enough to give me one, please let it be practical and dark so that I can put it on afterwards to go to the laboratory."

Summary:

Marie Curie is one of the most honored women in science; the first woman to be awarded a Nobel Prize, for her discovery of the radioactive element radium. Her initial successes came while working alongside her husband, an older scientist, but after he died in an accident, she successfully continued their work. Ironically, Marie Curie died because of the work that made her so famous; radium is a poisonous radioactive material which she repeatedly exposed herself to without being aware of the health consequences.

Vocab word: Cerebral, related to the intellect.
In her day, Marie Curie would have been considered uncommonly *cerebral* for a woman.

Themes: Not following the crowd, teamwork, self-determination and success

Facts:

Born in Poland to a family of teachers and educators; her father taught Math and Physics, two subjects that would figure prominently in Marie's later life.

Her family was not wealthy; they had lost many of their resources to patriotic Polish causes.

She fell in love with a brilliant young mathematician (who also loved her) but his family was opposed to their union - he came from money, and she was nearly penniless. These events had a lifelong emotional impact on the two of them.

After her relationship ended, Marie moved to France to study Physics, Chemistry, and Math at the University of Paris. She worked day and night to study and earn a living wage, proving her intense devotion to her studies.

She earned her degrees in 1893 (Physics) and 1894 (Math) and also began a relationship with an older science instructor, Pierre Curie. The two physicists soon were married and were inseparable, working side-by-side in their laboratory.

Her independent work with her husband would be very important to her as Marie was denied academic positions simply because she was a woman - despite her great intellect and her qualifications.

Around the turn of the 20th century, radioactive materials were an important topic of scientific investigation (although nobody had called them "radioactive" yet!). The Curies made a series of intriguing discoveries in this new field. However, both scientists (and the rest of the world) were unaware of the serious health risks of working with radioactive material.

Pierre, her husband, was accidentally killed by a vehicle in 1906. Though she was devastated by the loss, Marie continued her devoted scientific research.

After she made a breakthrough in the process of the isolation of radioactive materials, Marie refused to patent her accomplishment, allowing other scientists to freely pursue their research.

Marie Curie was the first woman to be awarded a Nobel Prize (in 1906), as well as the first person of either gender to win or share *two* Nobel Prizes (her second came in 1911). She is also the first and only woman to be buried in the Pantheon (resting-place of France's most highly-honored citizens) in Paris for her achievements.

Although the radioactive materials she worked with led to her great achievements, they also caused her death due to their highly toxic nature. Even to this day, her scientific notes and even her cookbook are too radioactive to be handled without protective gear.

Marie Curie's legacy is as a pioneering researcher and as an early feminist icon that fiercely pursued her career goals with no regard for naysayers or oppressive social rules about the role of women. To this day she continues to inspire young girls and women who have interests and talents in math and science!

Stephen Hawking (1942-present)

"My goal is simple. It is a complete understanding of the universe, why it is as it is and why it exists at all."

"However bad life may seem, there is always something you can do, and succeed at. While there's life, there is hope."

Summary:

Stephen Hawking is a brilliant theoretic physicist and astronomer who suffers from a serious degenerative disease that has left him confined to his wheelchair and unable to speak except through artificial means. He is living proof of the power of persistence and the strength of the human spirit. Apart from his inspiration contributions to theoretical physics, he has also authored books that put complicated scientific concepts into plain English – Hawking believes that even non-experts should have a solid understanding of science.

Vocab word: Undaunted, not discouraged due to difficulty or failure
Despite his degenerative disease, Steven Hawking is undaunted in his pursuit of scientific achievement.

Themes: Triumph over adversity, leadership in education, courage and conviction, determination

Facts:

Not a distinguished student, due to poor study habits, but he always had an interest in science, and his physics, his tutor recognized his talents from a young age.

Early in his career had to make a decision between observation and theory, and he chose theory.

While still a young man earning his Ph.D., Hawking began to experience symptoms of ALS or "Lou Gherig's Disease," which slowly destroys motor control.

Hawking also lost his ability to speak clearly as a result of the disease.

One of his scientist colleagues built him a small computer that Hawking could type into via small finger motions and have his speech rendered electronically.

Despite his many ailments, Hawking pioneered new ideas in Astronomy, and developed groundbreaking theories of black holes and the boundaries of the universe.

He is an extremely well-respected scientist and has been honored many times by his country and various scientific organizations.

Hawking's theory on extraterrestrial life is that "primitive life is very common and intelligent life is fairly rare."

Hawking was also the first quadriplegic to float in zero-gravity (on the "Vomit Comet," an airplane used to train and accustom future astronauts to zero-g conditions). This was the first time Hawking had experience free motion without his wheelchair in 40 years.

His stated reason for taking the flight? "I think the human race has no future if it doesn't go into space. I therefore want to encourage public interest in space," citing the dangers of nuclear war, wide-spread disease, and other dangers.

Hawking, who is also a popular scientific author, believes that "laypeople," or non-scientists, should have access to a clear understanding of science, and he writes many of his books in an accessible, simplified manner to encourage this understanding.

Essay Advice and Conclusion

So, you've picked your evidence (3 examples at a minimum, 5 is better)!

You've learned it inside and out.

What do you do now?

Well, one smart move would be to pick up a copy of my other SAT essay book, *Write The Best SAT Essay Of Your Life!* This book deals directly with the methods I use and teach my students. You can get it at eSATPrepTips.com.

Here's my quick advice about actually writing the SAT essay (these are the tricks I use to get a 12 every time):

1) Brainstorm the prompt: Pick a side, and spend 3 minutes at the beginning of the essay to map out exactly how your evidence best fits your thesis.

2) Use a five-paragraph structure: Don't get complicated here. Write a solid intro, three body paragraphs, and conclusion. If you're short on time, two body paragraphs will suffice.

3) Use your evidence: You've memorized it, so make sure to put down your impressive-sounding facts and specifics that prove you know what you're talking about!

4) Write a lot: It's a fact – the longer the essay, the better the odds of getting a perfect score. Aim to fill both pages if possible – it can be done!

5) Stay on topic: The only purpose of your essay is to support and prove your thesis and answer the question. Never wander off topic, even for a single sentence!

6) Proofread! Use the last seconds or minutes of your time to skim over your essay and look for obvious problems or mistakes in punctuation or spelling.

7) When you're done, forget about it: The essay is the first section of every SAT. Whether you think you aced it or bombed it, the important thing to do is get it out of your mind, and focus on the next section ahead of you.

8) Get a good night's sleep before the test!

The SAT essay rewards students who prepare in advance. Use this to your advantage and get the high score you deserve.

Relax – if you study your evidence, you'll be ready!

☺

Other SAT Prep books by Christian

Write The Best SAT Essay Of Your Life: Learn everything there is to know about the SAT essay section. Covers strategies, frequently-asked questions, important facts about the grading scale, and more. Contains a comparison and analysis of two actual SAT essays, including one that would receive a perfect score, and a list of essay prompts from previous tests. This book is worth hundreds of dollars of tutoring. Makes a great companion to *Top 30 Examples to Use as SAT Essay Evidence*.

Get your copy today at http://www.esatpreptips.com/write-the-best-sat-essay-of-your-life-a-guidebook/

SAT Grammar Crammer: Let's face it – nobody enjoys studying grammar, but it's important to get a great score on the SAT Writing section! This book was designed to quickly identify weak points and painlessly teach you the inner workings of the SAT grammar section. Hundreds of practice questions and 12 detailed yet concise lessons

Get your copy at http://www.esatpreptips.com/top-12-sat-writing-grammar-rules/

SAT Math Mastery Level 1: Perfect-Score Fundamentals: Written for students scoring 550 or below in Math. Review the essential Math basics that will be presented on the SAT. Many of these topics are from a long time ago; some go back to 4th and 5th grade. The problem isn't that these topics are *hard* for you – it's that you've totally forgotten that they ever existed. Let me lead you through practicing these easier fundamental topics.

Go to http://www.esatpreptips.com/sat-math-mastery-level-1-perfect-score-fundamentals-and-practice/

SAT Math Mastery Level 2: Tougher Tricks and Skills: A step up in difficulty from my previous math book, for students scoring between 500 and 700 on the Math section. Don't let fear of the unknown hold you back - practice intermediate to advanced SAT math skills and build on the work from Level 1.

Get it at http://www.esatpreptips.com/sat-math-mastery-level-2-tougher-tricks-and-skills/

Urgent Report on the SAT Critical Reading Section: A *FREE* instant download that provides immediate actions you should be taking starting *today* in order to ace the Critical Reading section. Don't wait – this information is extremely urgent and there's not a moment to waste – seriously!

Get it for FREE by joining my mailing list at http://www.esatpreptips.com/mailing-list/

Made in the USA
Lexington, KY
17 August 2013